DO902760

Innovative Exploration

Touring the Menlo Software Factory™

Innovative Exploration

Touring the Menlo Software Factory™

Second Edition

Written by the Menlo Innovations Team

Introduction by Rich Sheridan, Menlo CEO

Legend

Introduction

MENLO INNOVATIONS
software design and development

Welcome to Menlo Innovations.

Get ready for "different." We have given guided tours for years and this book was written in response to the popularity of those tours. I hope you enjoy your visit.

The Menlo Software Factory™ is located in the historic Kerrytown® District of Ann Arbor, Michigan, one of the older sections of Ann Arbor. Our building was built in 1899 and was originally a brick and oak beam warehouse.

Our company and its unique approach have been featured in Forbes magazine, the Wall Street Journal, and many other publications, both locally and nationally. Menlo has received numerous awards for our innovative work methods and team environment, including a spot on the 2007 Inc. 500 List of Fastest Growing Private Companies in America.

If you are intrigued by what you read in this book, and would like to see more, please contact us. We would be happy to schedule a tour!

Richard Sheridan,
Menlo Innovations' President & CEO

Introduction

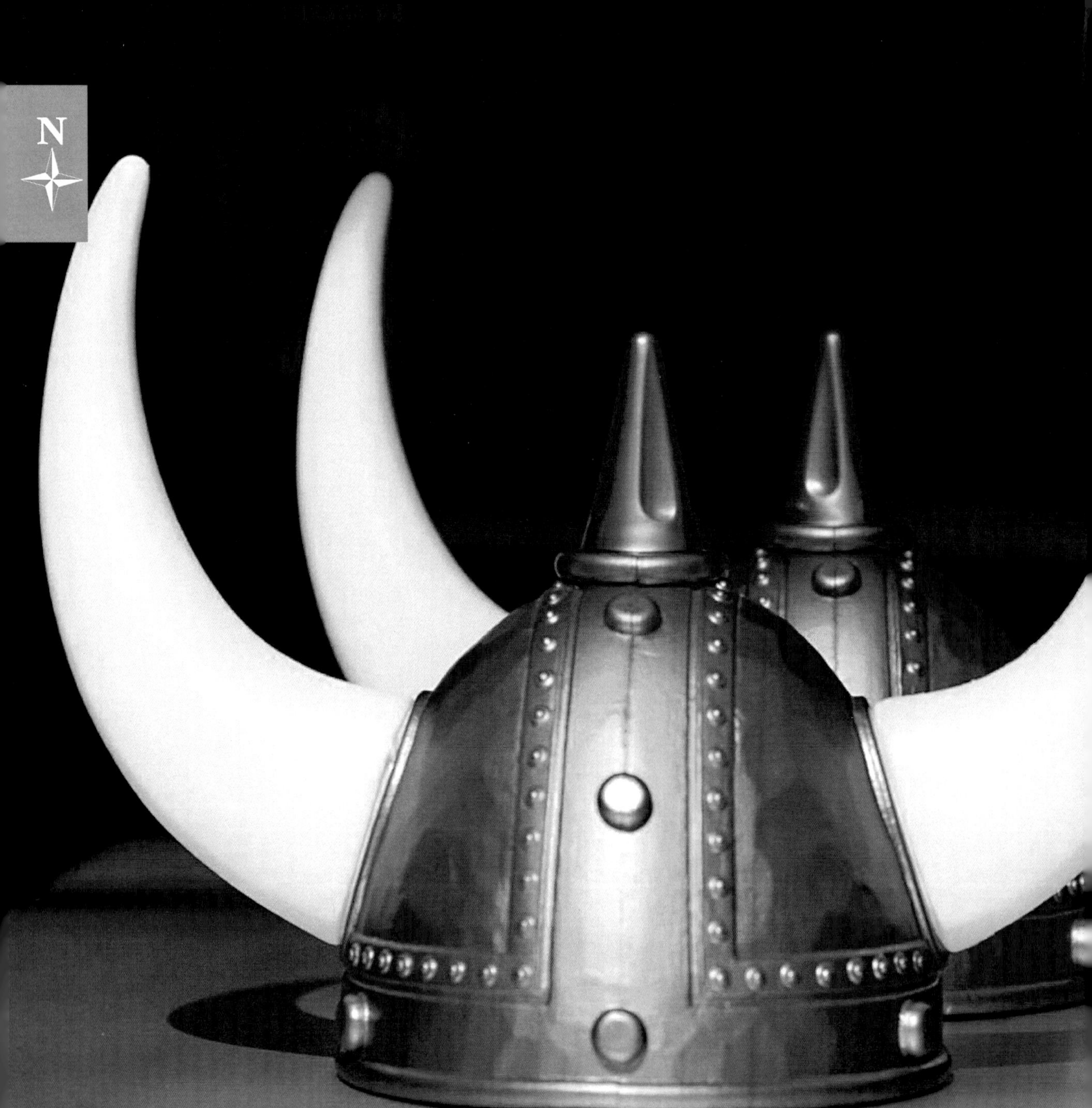

Menlo's Mission

Our mission is to:

"end human suffering in the world as it relates to technology™".

We pursue this mission by offering complete software design and development services to our clients. In the midst of these projects we focus on ending the long-standing suffering of three key stakeholders:

- Software project sponsors who traditionally have had little hope of steering projects to successful conclusion before money and executive patience is exhausted.

- End users of the software who, far too often, have no voice at all in the design yet must ultimately live everyday with decisions of people they have never met.

- The software teams themselves who typically labor under years of overtime, missed vacations, family celebrations, broken relationships and unrealistic expectations only to have the projects they work on never see the light of day.

Our goal since 2001 is to return the *joy* to one of the most unique endeavors in the history of mankind: inventing software!

The
Software Factory

Menlo Software Factory™

Menlo Innovations was inspired by the creative and productive work environment demonstrated at Thomas Edison's Menlo Park, New Jersey "Invention Factory." Like Edison, the driving factor behind everything Menlo does is to create useful and marketable products that deliver real business value.

The principles of the team environment that Edison established over 120 years ago still hold true today. Menlo has replicated his concept of a truly open and collaborative environment. All team members work side by side in a large open brick-walled workspace. No barriers (cubes, offices, or otherwise) limit communication within or between project teams. As Edison experienced, this fosters greater productivity and collaboration, in part, because people stop operating as individual heroes. Instead, the stream of thought and ideas proposed by one is improved upon by others among the team.

As the name suggests, Menlo Innovations is constantly generating and testing new approaches to solve the challenges with which the team is presented. With the strength of the collaborative ideas generated, the Menlo Software Factory™ team has not yet faced a problem they could not successfully solve together.

Often, the first word visitors say is "Wow." Upon opening Menlo's front door, people immediately hear the noisy conversations of team members discussing and working through the challenges of our client's projects.

Visitors see teams of people clustered around tables pushed together. Up close they notice two people working side by side at a single workstation, even sharing a keyboard and mouse.

The walls are covered with lots of index cards pinned to the wall. These cards hold the tasks and work assignments critical to advancing each project. In the spirit of Menlo's open and collaborative workspace, all of this information is posted for our entire team and our clients to see. Project identities are protected by fun and unique code names such as "Houlihan" and "Lancelot."

Despite what might appear to be chaos at first glance, there is a refined set of practices that drive all roles across the company, including developers, High-Tech Anthropologists®, quality advocates, and

project managers. At the heart of Menlo's methodology is the practice of "extreme programming" ("XP"), an iterative and incremental software development approach, first outlined in Kent Beck's "Extreme Programming Explained: Embrace Change."

Each task is captured on individual index cards and the team estimates the effort required to complete them. Project stakeholders then prioritize and schedule selected tasks. Finally, pairs of developers using a test first approach build the software components that correspond to the authorized tasks they have been assigned.

Upon even closer examination, you see Menlo's High-Tech Anthropologists® working within the same group of tables as our software developers. It is their work, and the unique relationship between these compassionate designers and our diligent programming team that creates the greatest value: software that is designed with the users at the center of the target.

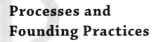

Processes and Founding Practices

At the heart of Menlo's success are the processes and practices that set the company apart from other firms. The founding principles of paired programming, test driven development, and requirements gathering through design have endured, but the philosophy of "make mistakes faster" has also inspired Menlo to adapt to new challenges as the company has grown.

The transparency around these practices not only allows new team members to come on board faster, but it encourages everyone to "own" the process and have a stake in each project's success. This culture fosters experimentation and discussion for improvements to existing process whenever anyone identifies a valid need.

The transparency found at Menlo is a benefit enjoyed by our clients. Early on in all client relationships stakeholders receive instruction as to how Menlo works. We teach the many points of

control clients have over the management of their projects. This clarity, including the power of "seeing" the proposed designs versus attempting to decipher the end product from pages and pages of specifications, allows clients to focus on aligning their decisions with business goals.

To ensure project success, Menlo employs techniques from across the technical and managerial spectrum: the Project Management Institute, Alan Cooper's user-centered design, Kent Beck's extreme programming and test-driven development, W. Edwards Deming's quality teachings, and much more.

This section serves as a high-level overview of our practices. We will highlight each of these as a standalone element; however it is the interconnection of them that make the Menlo Software Factory™ so successful.

Co-Location

What is co-location? Everyone on a common project team, including High-Tech Anthropologists®, developers, quality advocates, and project managers, sit together in one group. There are no separate offices, cubicles or other barriers that would hinder communication. All the tables, chairs, and computer hook-ups can be easily reconfigured to meet each of our client's changing resource needs. It is not unusual for the layout to be reconfigured for the addition of new projects, the completion of projects, or an adjustment in the size of an existing project.

Sitting adjacent to other project team member makes it easy to discuss ideas or challenges that arise. Many problems that would initiate an e-mail exchange or the scheduling of a meeting at another company are solved at Menlo by simply pushing chairs together for a few minutes or asking questions without even getting up.

The benefits of co-location are applicable not just for software development. For example, once elected, New York Mayor Michael Bloomberg implemented an open "bullpen" where dozens of aides and managerial staff are seated together in a large chamber. He recognized that the bullpen environment would "promote accountability and accessibility" across his team. Menlo wholeheartedly agrees!

an example
would be handy
right about now

Pairing

One of the core practices of the Menlo Software Factory™ is pairing, where two people work together on the same task. For example, Menlo developers share a single computer, keyboard, and mouse. While working together, one developer ("the driver") is coding while the other ("the navigator") is reviewing the work and suggesting where they should go next. High-Tech Anthropologists® when not at a computer, would trade the marker at the white board or the pencil while creating mock-ups.

Pairing enables collaboration on ideas and cross-pollination of project knowledge. Because each story card is always worked on by two people, the project is never held hostage by the knowledge of a single person. Other benefits of this practice are that it leverages peer accountability to reinforce adherence to the practices and provides a learning environment wherein pair partners continuously mentor each other.

Story Cards

At Menlo, tasks and project requirements for all team members are captured on 5" x 8" lined, index cards, called story cards. Each story card is independent and the collection of all stories describes the potential scope of a project. Cards are written to clearly define the business value and the impact to the target audience. An outline of the task to be completed, the desired output, and the definition of "done" are described as well. Cards are written so that any stakeholder, without translation, could understand both the business value and the task at hand.

Initial story cards for a project identify the target users' needs and create a high-level design path – including persona mapping, mock ups of the user interface, and assessments of the designs by target users. Often these are written by High-Tech Anthropologists® and project managers. As the project progresses, story cards are targeted more towards feature development and design refinement.

Story cards are prioritized with the sponsor during the weekly planning game, which drives the work authorized for the team. Because of their clarity and flexibility, discussions of trade-offs around task prioritization and reorganization are easy, and alternative development paths are quickly explored. Ultimately the power behind this system is the ability to make meaningful decisions for the project as a team.

Estimation

Most sponsors dream of managing a project with a budget that never runs out and a deadline that never comes too soon. The reality? Every project has constraints.

Estimating the amount of effort to complete each task allows the project manager to identify the associated cost. This helps to arm the sponsor with both the relative cost (budget) and the impact each feature would have on the timeline (deadline). Sponsors are better able to decipher which feature paths to prioritize.

During estimation, every pair on the team selects the amount of time they believe a particular task will take them to complete. They choose between 2, 4, 8, 16, 32 or 64 hours. The project manager then records the median within the set of estimates given by the team. The expectation is "an estimate is just an estimate." It is neither a guarantee nor a license to linger on the story card, but instead it is a challenge for each pair to try and meet or beat their estimate. The most important "estimating accountability rule" we have at Menlo is to inform your project manager whenever you feel your original estimate is at risk.

Show and Tell

At the end of each iteration, the project team assembles for a ritual we call "show & tell." This is an opportunity for the project sponsors to literally see the work the team has completed during the past iteration.

Show & tell generates value for the client in multiple ways:

1. It provides an open forum for discussions on functionality and changing needs, as our clients' worlds are always changing and their needs are never static

2. It builds a shared vision of the product being built, both within the stakeholder groups and across the Menlo project teams

3. It reinforces the planning process by demonstrating actual work completed on the story cards prioritized by the client the previous week, and provides context in which to guide planning for the upcoming week

4. It showcases the business value Menlo has generated for the client each week

The project manager typically acts as the master of ceremonies for the team, but all team members contribute to the show & tell presentation.

Planning Game

After the conclusion of the iteration's show & tell, the project manager partners with the client sponsors in an event called the planning game. You guessed it – during this activity the tasks for the upcoming weeks are selected and prioritized, thus providing a "steering wheel" for the clients to guide their project.

Often as the clients walk over to their first planning game, they quietly wonder, "Who has been making origami out of our story cards?" Planning at Menlo is a hands-on, high participation activity. Each story card that's to be considered for the plan has been copied onto regular paper, cut, and folded so that its size is relative to its estimate.

Next to the cards are rows of colored planning sheets organized on the table by week and by role. Each 11" x 17" sheet contains the outline of a box, which physically represents 40 hours of work for one pair (and the relative impact on the budget).

Together the project manager and clients select which tasks are of high priority. By placing the story cards on the planning sheets for all roles, the clients effectively authorize those tasks to be worked on within specific, upcoming iterations. The boxes on the planning sheets provide perimeters for time and budget.

As the project unfolds, planning games act as an instrument to discuss client business goals and considerations, such as:

· Feature selection

· Bug fixes

· What is in and what is out of scope

· Timeline of incremental releases

· Appropriate staffing levels for each iteration

· Impact on and projected end of the budget

The planning game is adjusted each week to both match the sponsor's highest priority needs and to strategically leverage our clients' resources (budget and time).

Work Authorization Board

In most environments, project management happens "behind-the-scenes." As a result, other team members don't understand what decisions are being made and why. At Menlo the project plan is not a secret, and is shared with the team first through the planning game. Using this information, the project manager constructs the project's work authorization board on a weekly basis, thus publicly presenting the project plan to all team members and stakeholders.

The transparency achieved with the work authorization board allows everyone on the team to see each pair's tasks and how they are prioritized within their lane. An estimate of how long each task will take to complete is written in the corner of each story card. Finally the current status of all tasks across the project is communicated using colored dots to indicate work that has been started, completed, blocked, ready for quality review or cancelled.

Ultimately the work authorization board fosters more effective communication across the team. The project manager is able to quickly and visually assess the status of the project, without hounding individual team members. Developers are able to identify what tasks may affect what they're coding, who is working on them, and when during the week the work will likely take place, all just by looking at the board.

In short, nothing is "behind-the-scenes" here. Everyone is empowered to help keep the project on track.

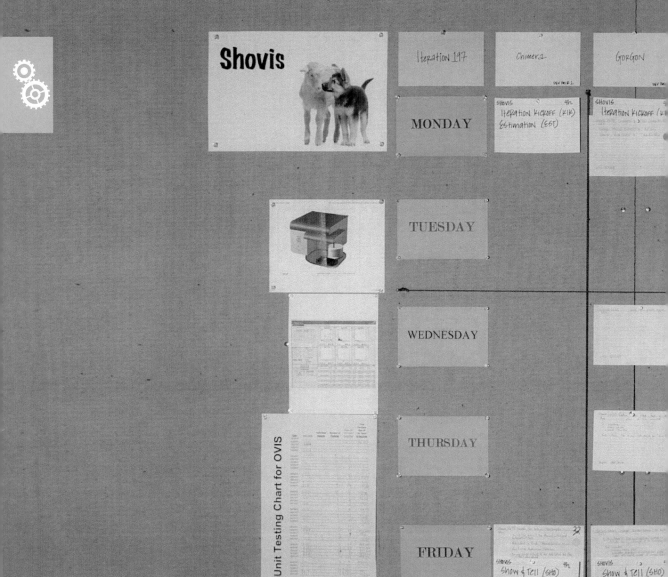

Shovis

Iteration 197 | Chimera | GORGON

MONDAY

SHOVIS 4h
Iteration Kickoff (KIK)
Estimation (EST)

SHOVIS
Iteration Kickoff (KI

TUESDAY

WEDNESDAY

Unit Testing Chart for OVIS

THURSDAY

FRIDAY

32
SHOVIS 4h
Show & Tell (SHO)
Planning Game (PLG)

SHOVIS
Show & Tell (SHO)
Planning Game (PLG

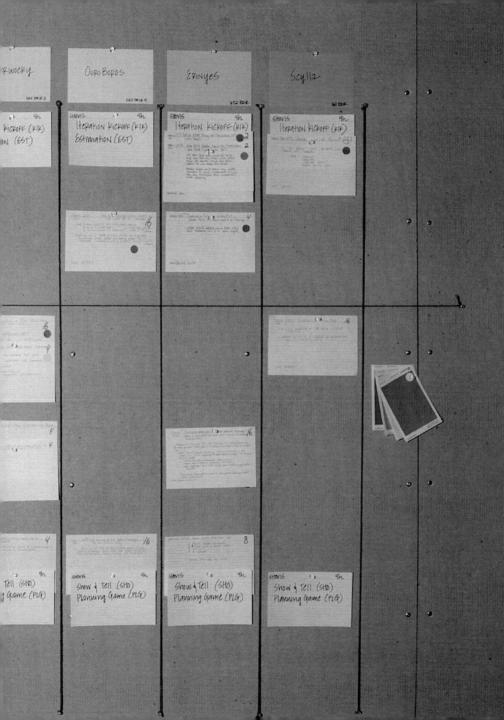

Reporting Status

Imagine being able to determine the exact status of any active task on your project in a single glance. No picking up the phone or tracking down individual team members ... simply take a look at the varying dots on the work authorization board.

The practice of dotting story cards originated just for this purpose. It enables both the team and sponsors to easily communicate and identify the progress of the project and pair within the team.

Whenever work has been started, completed, blocked, or cancelled a dot should be present. Menlo utilizes the following color code:

Yellow = the card is in progress

Red = work has been stopped and an explanation should be posted

Blue = the card has been cancelled

Orange = the QA/HTAs® need to review the completeness of the work

Green = the story card is officially done

Every team member strives for the green dot, which declares to the team – "We are done!"

Green Dotting

At Menlo, we know a story card is complete when a green dot is placed upon it.

There are two steps to the green dotting process. First, developers run a series of automated unit tests against their code, on their own computer. If all the tests pass, the developers then integrate their code into the current software application build on a separate integration machine and run the tests again. In all cases the tests must pass before the developers can move forward in the green dotting process.

Next a quick review of the work is done to identify any broken functionality and usability issues not caught by the unit tests. Looking at it from the user's perspective, High-Tech Anthropologists® test common scenarios and evaluate if the feature was built to the design specifications. QA in contrast utilizes exploratory testing to stress the new application functionality.

The process of "green dotting" always results in a conversation and action. These independent tests for "done" and the resulting conversations are critical to eliminating the challenge of what "done" means. Problems are caught before the developer pair moves on to their next story card, ensuring that no incomplete or "buggy" features are introduced into the software.

The Software Factory

Meetings at Menlo

Hanging on the wall In Menlo's workspace is a dart board with an alarm that sounds a chime each morning at 10:00 a.m. This is a call for all team members to gather in a circle for our daily stand up meeting. A team member grabs a token, one of our favorites is a viking helmet, and with their pair partner briefly describes for the group what they are working on and any problems they are encountering. Only the pair holding the token speaks during this meeting.

This is an abbreviated status update for the day. The meeting typically lasts only 13 minutes regardless of the number of attendees. The pace of the meeting is quick and the pairs are concise in describing their work. Questions can be asked of the team, but they are answered on an individual basis after the meeting adjourns. Once the last pair gives their update, the meeting concludes with an inspirational "Let's be careful out there!"

But what if someone needs help from the team and stand-up has already taken place that day? The team member in need just shouts a "Hey Dawson!" if it is Dawson project specific, or "Hey Menlo!" if the question is applicable company wide. Immediately team members stop what they're doing and shout back, "Hey {insert name of team member here}!" and the meeting commences. People don't even need to move from their seats and the meeting concludes as the question is quickly answered.

Menlo's Culture

Introduction to Menlo's Culture

At Menlo, it's our team that sets us apart. As a consulting company, we strive to provide a great design and end product. However, if all we did was develop a great user interface, we'd consider that a failure. Our greatest successes are clients who have implemented new problem solving strategies in their own organizations, based on the innovative and collaborative culture they've experienced at Menlo.

What's the secret to Menlo's influential culture? The first step is to ensure that we have the right people on our team. Above and beyond the specific skill sets and experiences someone might bring, we look at kindergarten skills. In the interview process we strive to answer the following questions: Do you play well with others? Do you share? Are you curious? Do you put away the crayons when done coloring?

From there, team members enter an environment where constant learning and mentoring pervade all we do. We set high expectations for team members to live out our processes daily. Individuals are also encouraged to give feedback as we continuously improve our practices. Just as individuals or pairs on the team can always improve their skills, we recognize that Menlo can always improve the way we do things.

In any company, teaching and challenging each other can be difficult. Coworkers are much more likely to receive constructive feedback if they trust the person who is delivering the message.

Menlo team members work to enhance their "communication toolkit" to tailor their delivery for each co-worker. These soft skills are just as important as the technical skills. To drive success in our consulting we must connect with and influence those around us. Simply stating "I'm right, do it this way" won't cut it at Menlo Innovations.

Instead, Menlo team members aim to influence those around them. This is easier said than done. It takes more effort to let your partner experience small challenges and patiently steer them towards success, than it does to simply tell them the "right" answer in the first place. Although everyone naturally wants to be successful in all situations, we recognize that working through a small struggle today will result in a better understanding of how to approach challenges in the future. This perspective looks towards long term success, as opposed to a short-sighted view of the present alone.

We apply this concept to our consulting relationships with clients as well – we

want them to be transformed by their experiences here. Thus we immerse our clients in the team, which gives them the opportunity to work alongside Menlonians right here in "The Factory™." It naturally exposes them to our culture and practices on a daily basis. Our clients aren't "told" what to do. Through problem solving together, clients both see and experience firsthand the effectiveness of Menlo's processes. Those who have personally worked through a challenge here are much more apt to adopt what they've learned, than those who only hear about it.

In the end, the secret to our culture comes down to leadership. What does this look like at Menlo? We believe leadership is not hierarchical, rather it can occur from anywhere on the team. The best type of leadership is that which helps those around you produce better results than they would on their own. Whether it is for our pair partner this week, the co-worker on another project, our sponsor, or the company as a whole, we work to help others succeed.

Class Names - Starts w/Captial letter
Unit
Test Class -
Helper TestClass -
Interfaces
Methods -
Fields -
and finish w/camelcase
Properties - treat like
Variables /arguments - start w/lower case
TestMethods -

Let's Run the Experiment: A Formula for Culture

Visitors are often intrigued when they see babies in our workplace, evidence of Menlo's willingness to adapt our culture. At one time, two Menlonians were on maternity leave, with a third anticipating the birth of her child at the end of the year. Each wanted to return in some capacity, the question remained, "How?"

One of the moms planned to return full time after leave, but felt her daughter was too young to enter day care. Another mom wanted to stay-at-home, but maintain flexibility to earn some extra income. The third enjoyed the problem solving and people development discussions that weren't likely to occur with an infant.

The three brainstormed potential solutions with co-owners Rich and James. Rich suggested, "Bring your baby to work." The quick response was, "What? That will never work. This is a big, open, and shared space, with lots of cords and expensive equipment. Where would we put the babies?" (Even Rich acknowledges that he had a moment of hesitation.)

He realized the baby could sit right next to the mom, because, "hey, she's not going anywhere." If she fusses, his mom can pick her up and comfort her. The reality is that the team was often found holding the baby!

When trying something new you never know how it will work. The experiment worked. You'll still find a baby or dog around on most days; proof of Menlo's questioning of conventional wisdom to improve the way we do business. Many teams often avoid change out of fear of what might go wrong. At Menlo, one of our favorite phrases is, "Let's run the experiment."

Players on Menlo's Team

Menlo's team is more like a baseball team than a traditional business team with managers, directors, and reporting relationships. For example, the pitcher does not report to the catcher on a baseball team. They each have unique talents and responsibilities and it's the relationship between those roles that makes the team work rather than an organization chart defining a hierarchy.

Our team consists of project managers, software developers, High-Tech Anthropologists®, quality advocates, and the factory floor manager. These roles require different talents and skills and have different responsibilities within our process. Each of these roles advocate for different stakeholders or aspects of the project:

- Project managers advocate for the sponsor of the project
- Software developers advocate for technology and the computer
- High-Tech Anthropologists® advocate for the end users of the system being built
- Quality advocates advocate for "fit for purpose"
- The Factory Floor Manager advocates for the health of the team

While working in the Menlo Software Factory™, each team member can hold only a single position. That is, project managers cannot also be developers or High-Tech Anthropologist®. This is by design because we want there to be spoken conflict between the roles when appropriate. It is in this spoken conflict where our process produces the greatest value.

High-Tech Anthropologist®

We wholeheartedly believe the most expensive type of project failure is having built software that no one ever uses. A close second? Software that is usable only by power users as opposed to the audience for which it was originally intended.

To avoid these failures, the High-Tech Anthropology® team researches what make users successful in their interactions with an application. We use the term "anthropologist" quite deliberately.

The only way to understand what would make a new system successful is to study and observe its potential end users in their native environment. This includes gaining an understanding of the differences between users of the software, the kinds of mistakes each are prone to make, and how those differences should drive the design.

With an empathetic approach in mind, High-Tech Anthropologists® have a self-stated goal: **"to end human suffering in the world as it relates to technology™."** They gather requirements

by actually designing potential solutions and checking their design assumptions with representative users. This team includes experienced business analysts as well as those versed in the nuances of user interface design tools and techniques. In the process of creating a successful solution, High-Tech Anthropologists® utilize techniques such as job shadowing, personas, use cases, hand-drawn screen mock-ups, object models, workflow assessments, and high-level screen designs to ensure that the user's needs are met.

High-Tech Anthropologists® design, write story cards to outline implementation of the designs, and act as translators for both the users and the developers.

Developers

Here's a window into the life of a software developer at Menlo, revealing what sets them apart. The team at Menlo writes code using a weekly iterative and incremental approach. Working from story cards, as do the other team members at Menlo, developers employ a test-first/ test-driven design. This ensures that the code in the current software application build is covered by automated unit tests. The practice also adheres to the tenets of object-oriented design and development. Their code typically has 95% code coverage by unit tests. New pair partners are assigned weekly, which helps ensure that code is critically reviewed as it is being written.

This test-driven development approach means our projects have a stronger architecture, fewer bugs, and a more flexible system for adding new functionality and its impact on the core product. Pairing and repairing ensures rapid transfer of knowledge and no singular dependency on a "tower of knowledge" that could ultimately threaten the success of the project.

Menlo's software developers have worked in a variety of languages including Java, C^{++}, C$^{\#}$, ASP, and Javascript. They've also worked on Windows, Macintosh and Unix platforms, and with a variety of web servers, application servers, and database servers. However, we believe technology selection should not be based on what the programmers enjoy most or what they're most familiar with, but instead on how the technology choices support the business objectives.

Quality Advocate

The charge of the quality advocates at Menlo is to evaluate if the software we create is truly "fit for purpose." We don't just want to create software that meets the original specifications, we want to assess along the way if the design and implementation are satisfying the needs of users while also supporting the business goals of the client.

A key activity of the quality advocate team is to engage in exploratory testing beyond what any automated test suite could accomplish. This may take the form of build testing or simply reviewing the product for bugs with an eye to identify usability issues. Quality advocates play a critical role in green dotting and reviewing whether the individual features coded by developers are "done."

Although everyone on the team should keep the big picture of the project in view this is our quality advocate's primary responsibility. This involves staying plugged into kick off meetings, estimation discussions, sponsor show and tells, planning meetings, and impromptu problem solving conversations. Quality advocates focus on knowing what types of questions to ask when problem solving, when to ask, and whom they should ask. This again is a valuable contribution to any project.

Quality advocates support the team by asking questions and challenging others to consider the consequences of varying design paths. They help clients measure risk as it applies to the quality of the product, and measure how closely the product meets the quality goals as set forth by stakeholders.

Project Manager

As if viewing the project through the eyes of the client, project managers at Menlo consider the impact on scope, schedule, and budget with every decision they make. The PM is assigned as the sponsor's advocate and partners with them to identify business goals and prioritize upcoming work. In parallel, they support the team through translating the impact of project constraints, so that team members are freed up to focus on their specific objectives. The PM also works to remove barriers which may limit the team's progress and to facilitate collaboration between the team and the client.

However, the PMs role also facilitates communication within the group of stakeholders. This may include helping stakeholders identify where they disagree over the project's direction, assisting in the creation of an agreed upon vision or discerning subtle but substantive challenges the client is trying to overcome. In response the project manager, with support from the team, is responsible for proposing alternative solutions at varying costs.

The PM role strikes a balance between customer relations and Menlo's iterative and incremental approach to project management. On a weekly basis the PM prepares and facilitates iteration kick off, estimation, show and tell and planning game. The PM keeps the project board up to date, provides team members with authorized story cards, keeps track of the established budget, and more. A PM's work never ends...

Factory Floor Manager

As you can imagine, there are many moving parts at Menlo, all of which change on a weekly, basis. The Factory Floor Manager is dedicated to asking and answering the key questions around resource management, people development, training and sales support, and compilation of invoicing data. Some of those questions are:

- What roles are needed to support this client and in what quantity?
- What challenges does each team face this week and do project managers have specific resource requests to address them?
- Are there pairing opportunities for cross-training, knowledge transfer, and mentoring to be considered for assisting in skill development across the team?
- Who has requested time off and how will that affect resource planning?
- Are there team members who have stood out in their performance and contribution to the team, who should be considered for more leadership?

One artifact produced by the Factory Floor Manager is the "Resource Plan," which communicates the project and pairing assignments for the coming week. Each of the above questions is considered when creating this schedule. In this way, and many others, the Factory Floor Manager has a direct hand in building the "learning organization" that is the Menlo Software Factory™.

Our Clients

Creating value is our passion. All projects at Menlo engage with external clients who have come to Menlo with a request to solve a problem. Sometimes the challenge is how to successfully break into a market with a new product. It may be to gain a new perspective and corresponding toolkit to influence cultural change within an organization. Other times it is to take an existing product and give it a more valuable and intuitive user interface.

The clients who Menlo attracts are seeking a partnership. From the start, we identify the common vision and business goals together. Clients participate in a brief training on Menlo's processes to empower them in their role as "stakeholder." Through our iterative approach, project sponsors at Menlo are in a unique position – the true state of a project is exposed at each weekly show and tell meeting. Thus planning decisions for the upcoming week are based on the most up-to-date picture of the project.

Our process creates transparency which can at times create discomfort. Our goal is to build the solution that our clients need. Every project has budget, timeline, and scope limitations. Menlo recognizes that at times hard decisions need to be made. We prepare our clients to make the best possible choice by presenting alternative solutions and making the tradeoffs clear. In this way, we make decisions together and give the project the best chance for success.

And then there is you ... our reader

First of all, allow me to thank you for making the investment of time to learn more about the Menlo Software Factory™. My guess is that if you've gotten to this page, you appreciate the importance and value of returning joy to creating software, and you, like me, have been searching for better ways of doing things than are customary.

Above all else, I hope that this "virtual tour" of Menlo has provided you with inspirational ideas to meet the challenges you face. Please know that you are welcome here any time. It is very easy to schedule a tour or a "Menlo Experience" visit. We offer many free seminars and webinars, as well as formal classes in our methods.
We learn something about ourselves each time we teach our methods to others. We *LOVE* to teach as we believe a rising tide floats all boats. We want others to experience the joy we experience every day.

Obviously, I'd be remiss if I didn't say that we would be delighted to be part of the effort to design and build the software you envision will change the world!

Ask Rich

?

Ask Rich

**1. Did you guys think this up yourselves?
How did you figure all this out?**

For a good portion of my career, I was very frustrated with the results
of the teams that I was a part of or that I managed. I was convinced
there was a better way of doing things than was customary and was
determined to find it. I had no idea what I was looking for so I began
reading books about management, team work, and organizational
development. For example, Peter Senge's book, "The Fifth Discipline:
The Art and Practice of Learning Organizations" had a profound impact
on my thinking.

The seminal moment for me was in 1999, when I was reading Kent
Beck's wiki on extreme programming and saw a video on a company
in California called IDEO. I now had the vision for what I was looking
for. From 1999 until now it has simply been a series of continuous
improvements influenced by many other sources such as Deming,
Cooper, Gladwell, and of course Mr. Edison has been a constant
source of inspiration.

2. How do you convince people to pay for pairing?

All of our efforts to sell Menlo's services have been a result of a very thoughtful and intentional education-based marketing effort. Our tours, for example, are an excellent way to begin the education process. It's amazing how many people "get it" right away when they see pairing in action. What they see is constant communication, collaboration, and a steady effort being applied the entire time they are here. Most then recall times in their own careers when they've had a similar productive experience when working with someone else. When I remind them of the cost of quality issues in software projects, they begin to connect the dots on how powerful this approach can be. Finally, I point out that while we have been doing software design and development since our inception in 2001, we do not have a "help desk" or a "support line." We certainly don't claim to be perfect, but it is pure joy to build software that works reliably and doesn't require the constant attention to bug fixing that plagues most software teams.

3. How do you get used to the noise?

It's funny that our team is at the point when they are most bothered when the room is too quiet rather than too noisy. Newcomers report that it usually takes about three weeks to acclimate to the noisier environment. The brain is an amazing filter.

4. How do you find people who like to work in this environment?

I would say it starts with the same education-based marketing that we use to attract potential customers. People who are interested in working here usually start with a tour or one of our many free seminars. Those that are intrigued by what they see drop off their résumé and then are ultimately invited to our next Extreme Interviewing™ event. This style of interviewing gets us a lot of attention from authors, national magazines, and conferences. It is described fully in a white paper available on our website. The main goal of our interviewing practice is to specifically seek those candidates who are "good kindergarteners."

5. How do you estimate the size of a project at the beginning?

The secret to doing this is our time-tracking system, where every person turns in a timesheet once a week detailing the time they spent working on each storycard. These actual "actuals", when aggregated, give us an excellent ability to compare potential projects against projects we've worked on in the past. This gives us an ability to generate early size ranges for these potential projects using analogous estimating techniques. We then spend time at the beginning of a new project doing a bottom-up estimate to refine our initial size range.

6. Is it true that you don't write documentation?

It is true that the requirements documents we write are different (and we believe more powerful) than the shelfware documents that are common amongst most traditional teams. Our first level of documentation is the wallboard displays of work authorization and status. Our handwritten storycards and related foamcore boards, depicting screen designs, represent documentation that is actually used to drive the team to results. Our programmers create automated unit testing frameworks that are required to be up to date with the latest code base, and that reflect the design and architectural decisions being made by the programmers. The power of automated unit tests is in their ability to immediately flag a violation of a previous design decision. No shelfware document has that ability.

In regards to end-user documentation, our overarching goal is to avoid creating software that needs it. The specialty of our High-Tech Anthropology® team is in creating highly usable and useful software for the target end-user audience, rather than the programmers who built the software.

Ask Rich

7. Does this process scale?

The Menlo Software Factory™ is built to accommodate a team of up to 100 people. Using these methods we have successfully run projects with 30-40 team members and multiple projects run in the same space. Corporate teams of several hundred to several thousand have taken our training classes and have adapted our methods for these larger teams.

8. What's your attrition rate?

In the spirit of Jim Collins' book "Good to Great", our focus has always been to get the right people on the bus and the wrong people off the bus. Thus we spend very little time measuring attrition. That said, when I'm asked about attrition rates I like to say that Menlo has a "negative attrition rate" because many of those who leave Menlo (for various reasons), frequently return. In this way Menlo is more like an open bird cage than a ball and chain.

By using pairing in the Menlo Software Factory™, we're able to leverage the skills and knowledge of the whole team in such a way that no single individual bottlenecks the productivity of the team. Even better, no individual is trapped in a prison of knowledge and unable to move to new projects and new technologies because knowledge is cross-pollinated throughout the team.

9. What do you do when two people don't get along?

My favorite response when asked this question is, "What do you do?" At least in our environment, when two people don't get along we know it right away. In traditional office environments it's possible to have people fighting for months or years and never know it. We often say about Menlo that we have all the same problems that everyone else has but our system discovers those problems sooner so we can deal with them while they're still small.

10. What's the deal with the Viking helmets?

First of all, they're just fun and we think that "fun" is an important part of innovation. The Viking helmets also have a practical use in our process. Our daily standup meeting is controlled by a token and the token is most often the Viking helmet. A two-handled token is convenient for a team that works in pairs. In this way each pair grabs hold of one of the horns, introduces themselves, and updates everyone on their status. Finally, team members often bring their children into the workspace and the kids enjoy donning the helmets.

Thanks Menlo!

As with all things at Menlo, we struggle with putting an "author's name" on this book as there were so many people who contributed directly and indirectly. It is unfair that my name is most closely associated with Menlo. I am the one who does much of the public speaking around the world and thus my persona is that of leader and visionary CEO. However, everyone at Menlo contributes to the passion and enthusiasm for what we do and the fingerprints of the whole team are on every part of our process, as they are with this book.

Thanks to my business partners and co-founders James Goebel and Bob Simms, without whom Menlo would not be possible. Thanks to Lisamarie Babik, our resident evangelist, to getting the book process started and being a contributor along the way. Thanks especially to Carol Sheridan and Christina Carmichael who did the lion's share of the heavy lifting to get the project done. Thanks to Ryan Slone for layout and graphics support and Ryan Pletzke for photography.

Finally, thanks to all Menlonians, past and present for helping create such a fun, compelling environment for doing hard work!

410 N. Fourth Ave
3rd Floor
Ann Arbor, MI 48104

734 • 665 • 1847

info@
menloinnovations.com